po zapomenutých kolejích,podél

ravy, které mu dlouho bránily ve výjezd do širého kraje

sto se zpolečn ztrácelo v dálce,skryté

. Jen   se ukazoval nad obzorem střechami domů,

ch komínů a kříži zvonic. Jedno   předměstí   hoře

odnášel vítr. Roztahoval se   celé nebi jako rozví

hříva.

tor a Samděvjatov seděli na podlaze   Samděvjatov celou dobu něco vysvět

Andrejevičivi ukazoval do dálky rukou. Chvílemi

                                              nic slyšet. Jur

znova ptal. Anfim Jefimovič přibližoval   tvář k

aže se křikem, opakoval řečené mu přímo do

To zapálili   Gigant.   Tam se   junkeri,

li. Vůbec   ještě neskončil. Vidíte černé tečky na zvo

ši.   odtamtud Čechy."

    nic nevidím. Jak to všechno

A támhleto   hoří Chochriky,řemeslnické předměstí.   K

    obchodní lánky je stranou. Proč mě to zajímá.

                                 Do centra města se zatí

říkám centrum - centrum města.   ,knihovna. Naš

Jan Zábrana
The Lesser Histories

MODERN
CZECH
CLASSICS

Jan Zábrana

Jan Zábrana
THE LESSER HISTORIES

Translated by Justin Quinn

Karolinum Press

A catalogue record for this book is available
from the National Library of the Czech Republic.

This poetry collection was first published in Czech as *Stránky z deníku*
by Československý spisovatel in 1968. In 2020,
Host published its comprehensive *Jan Zábrana: Básně a povídky*;
this English translation, however, was started earlier and is based
on the edition of *Stránky z deníku* that appeared in *Básně*,
a collection of three books of Zábrana's poetry, published by Torst in 1993.

Cover and frontispiece photo courtesy of photo archive Torst, 2022

ISBN 978-80-246-4933-7
ISBN 978-80-246-4934-4 (pdf)
ISBN 978-80-246-4935-1 (epub)
ISBN 978-80-246-4936-8 (mobi)

Move then with new desires,
For where we used to build and love
Is no man's land, and only ghosts can live
Between two fires.
Cecil Day Lewis

Poetry without junk is boring.
(Básnictví bez veteše je nuda.)
Vítěslav Nezval

PART I

SUMMER 1944

The season's last horse races. They're off!
The fall, the finish... That day a card
for him from S... A dog howls of
the war, and smells the knacker's yard.

The Great Dictator on release.
His father honeys the tobacco.
July! A heat that's full of ice.
Assassinations. Miracles also.

From the butcher shop of Omaha,
the SS Argonauts withdraw.
Sterbe, Erika.... sterbe wohl...

The baths. Hay fever. Cyrillics stain
the surface... Now, once more, in vain:
not thus in Russian, not at all.

DEAD GIRL REMEMBERED

It's ever closer now, the star
that saw the urnfield culture passing.
Back then it shone down from afar
on the local girl, dead at the crossing.

Innocence shrives the guilt to come:
it chooses and whites out the graves
of people who will leave behind them
nothing – a few stones, scattered staves.

The future simply loses sight
of them – tossed from quick carriages,
raped by drunk uncles, crushed by trains.

There's just some pubic bones, picked white
in clay, in ditches where dogs piss,
on throughways with the stink of foreskins.

SPLENDID ISOLATION DESTROYED

Alone. At sea. It seemed to lie on
the waters like a dream that drew you,
an island that was called Jan Mayen.
Europe and war meant nothing to you.

You loved it, wandering up the steps.
White peas go clattering in the bath.
Then Germans from the Eastern steppes –
two lines along the muddy path.

And in the kitchen Georgian girls
horsed round and whipped up ice-cream curls.
The dead draped on a van, a car.

Jan Mayen Island gradually
went floating off, lost in the sea,
and lost among those days of war.

13

KHLESTAKOV ARRIVES FOR HARVEST HOME, SUMMER 1945

Lots of new widows to go round.
They scrubbed until the floors were shiney.
And in the woods a keeper found
a shred of letter: *Lieber Heini!*

A cousin called: 'Come on back home!
The cellar!' Villages stank of spirit.
He jingled in his pocket some
gold teeth (German), and near it,

on the green, music set the mood:
The big shot's here! His driver's curse.
Warm greetings, cheers, some honest food,

the national costume (somewhat worse
for wear). All heard him softly soughing:
'The first free harvest is *now in*.'

EVENING TRAINS

The evening trains went hooting by
the factories and the fields of wheat.
Harmonicas would lilt and sigh
songs such as 'Путъ далек лежит'…

in the year of nineteen forty-five,
in that year of first cigarettes,
when farms without a soul alive
gave hope – like red sunsets.

The evening trains made their way fast
to Prague and to new dizziness.
The weekend gone, I jumped a carriage

and left, the landscape rolling past.
Along the line of that express
youth fell away – a head of cabbage.

SUBLET

That evening he returned and all
was as he'd left it. The ceiling white…
But something in it now was bright
and empty. He even failed to fall

or trip as usual on the way
inside. Stripped off his clothes. Then aired
the rooms. She was out. His coat shared
the same hook as hers yesterday.

Some books (not his). And smokes. Forsake her?
Her children all gone to their Maker.
And then? He'd nowhere else to go.

The radio next door. No takers
but him, surprised to finally know.
He'd walked long miles through mud and snow.

PRAGUE FALL

The fogs came wandering in and covered
the still warm sleeper in the morning.
Fogs round the chimney, and on its warning
signs the butterflies lit and shivered.

Fair days toward evening, another mart:
tremor of lashes and kohled ridges,
and calls of 'Such shy partridges!'
that got the dance off to a start.

Like a doctor, the alarm clock on the pulse.
Saturday. The city loud with bells
for weddings. Taxis whipped by wind.

Was itching to get dressed. I saw
the serious drinkers, waiting, raw,
outside the pubs, for their first pint.

FOR A DEAD GIRL

The clink of streetcars fades and dies.
Who went into that darkness later
for good, like grief? The perpetrator.
She'd long gone to paradise.

Her mother to this day still plinks
piano keys – 'Who did for her?' –
in some big villa. Logs of fir
and oak hauled into its precincts.

Her hair bright cilia: that jaunt
outside the town, alive it flashed,
when love led to her nemesis.

When every day the 'old world' crashed
and burned, a world she didn't want,
that couldn't have interested her less…

YOUNG OVIDS SAY FAREWELL

And autumn again. The women's limbs
departed here beautifully bronzed,
and just the lifeguard's fish-hook swims
off from the deck across the pond.

These last few weeks the sound of jazz.
In shops, pink nylons are displayed,
fragrant and flashing, like music played
through parks, like a river through a sluice.

And still these young men hear those strains.
And horses race on Chuchle Downs.
And still the motor drowns them out.

Cologne behind her ears. She pouts
and prinks through these weeks' aimless drift.
It's halted by the general draft.

For Jiří Kolář

DECEMBRISTS

Like us they dreamed their dreams of pastures new
but had to find a path through rough earthwork.
The Summer Garden was their preferred purlieu,
for its leaf canopies above the Kronverk.

There they took poison beneath the statuary's lime,
and shadowed by the trees built in a blur
their airy castles – this for the final time
when *Nayabur* ceded to *Dekabur*.

Jack-in-the-Box. Strike a match and blow.
As feelings like panaches skyward beat.
You voices in apartments, home you go,

the long way round down dark side-streets.
The empties strewn about – Château Lafite,
and even here and there some Veuve-Clicquot.

THE PETRASHEVSKY CIRCLE
AS A LIVING TRADITION

All goes well for the person who
wishes well… House heat exchanged
for snow, he leaves as after curfew
to meet with friends as they've arranged.

Below, shoemakers earn their bread.
The image of the Petrashevskys
is glued and hammered in the head –
betrayed, convicted, sent to freeze.

While in the disciplinary distance
they've been forgiven long ago.
They're still admired for their persistence.

And like a threat to their resistance,
the moon sends moonshine down and snow
to hide the truth of their existence.

CHILDHOOD BUREAU

If you shed tears for a fine topboot
found moulding in an oubliette,
if castles make you catch your breath,
always hopeless, boding death,

if books like *The Volcano's Crater*
scare you more than some dull critter,
if you work childhood like a job,
annoyed each day by its fey charms,

you'll miss the chickens' song, its throb
from women's palms along their arms.
Toward evening delirium could

touch even you… But you feel good
the moment that the ears of corn
from green to gold begin to turn.

VILLAGE CIRCUS

And the big old bear is shedding hairs.
The horses spavined, zebras too.
A lad in rags begs at the doors
for honey, herbs or what have you.

Like members rise for love, the tent
goes up beyond the village, new
for those who from all parts descend
when they make out the hullabaloo –

buffoons who beat their belly flitch,
and dogs unmuzzled chase a bitch.
At night it's full. Some hulking swain

blows on a shining bugle – the pitch
like that of frogs in field and lane,
or the canvas flapping in the rain.

WITCH BURNING I

The April night... Will the groom come?
Shame as the resined broomsticks thresh
in wheels of flame. And further shame
as on a thread. Shame in the flesh.

Mystery in all. As twilight loomed
the barren spells of magic fled.
And green oh green the clover bloomed,
the purple not yet through it spread.

The girls cleave to the shades of trees,
'can stay up late, just as they please.'
The small kids run up hangman's hill.

And thighs of women blazing past.
Firebrands for children! Innocents will
destroy such comely idols best.

WITCH BURNING II

The chilled-through cruelty still awaits
the first shout, as for a fine silk shawl,
like those old ones for rain like rods.
So flame came whipping from them all.

Like that time, flesh is broiled alive,
the reek still here today — flesh burns,
sweet body's flesh that can't survive
the torment, cooled then by lucernes.

They still believe that death shrives sin,
that monks know most about women.
I stood there. Watched the flames retouch

the sky with signs of youth, all new.
And you who I loved oh so much —
who were they burning there but you!

PSALM

A psalm about the ways wind blows,
a psalm of lick-spit bend and scrape,
a psalm for the disappeared, for those
who are 'shot while trying to escape,'

about how horses, broken, pull,
about how barbed wire like a forest
grew round the house, and that *hard* pearl
in conscience – the day you felt it first,

a psalm of cruelty in utopians,
sung to pistons' closings and openings,
a psalm for the silent and their tears,

and owl song drowned by asses' cheers,
a psalm that maybe from their snare
flies like a bird into the air.

For Bedřich Fučík

JOURNEYMAN YEARS

An unknown town. The hot day done.
As for lodgings, around here none.
On roadsides lie the golden days
of dreams and sweat-soaked tennis shoes,

while June is cradling in itself
July with something like resolve.
Old poems mere shadows of themselves –
they'd like new clothes, oh *something else!*

But how those poems still go for gold!
And in that summer he recalled
the springtime, full of bright and clear

good spells and portents – here, right here.
That spring to which his mind returned,
its souls now gone, its bodies mourned.

PART II

A SENTIMENTAL JOURNEY

From one man to the next she stretched
her hair much like a clothesline. Chased
by med students, her game was pitched
to what alone would please him best.

Before the thread's end that she'd sown,
before kohlrabis turned to wood,
Could Šomková have dreamt or known
the poet that he was?...Nor could

she ever. She led him in a circle,
while he hoped for a miracle.
By the fence, she mocked: 'Give it your all!'

Skirting the apple trees and cherries,
she wanted it. Going for the berries,
she sought out lips, and cried, 'The ball!'

ORIGIN

Toy cars, oh yes, the rod unspared,
cod-liver oil, bad habits, scouts.
The pedagogical muse turfed out
eternally half read, half heard,

but ready… And still they forced him on her:
a pic from Lány, patria a trap
for those who teach the children honor
(no venery! no theft!). This chap

was one more of the fat-faced brats
who never hung out with the lads.
A thousand despot governesses

can't prep you for a knock-out: ten,
nine, eight… Yet up he gets again —
the boxer's fascinating progress.

BIO (SHORT VERSION)

A grandson! For him the village women –
old, in black – make sacrifices.
Stench in the yard. All crowded in.
The smallest ailment paralyzes

him, now eighteen. In Prague there's snow
and show trials. Buys some gabardine –
it's from two Christmases ago.
And then the married woman. Scene:

the doorway: 'My dear!' (his and hers).

Only Czech Rail pensioners
continue to believe the stars
and buy timetables every year,
though they're eternally stuck here.
going nowhere, ever. No-one stirs.

BARBERS

The old lads said, at home the walls
they built themselves, but mostly skill
in our town meant that you would haul
spuds to a still… The local school?

There wasn't one. No bricks to build it.
The state? If you don't fleece it, you
fleece your own family. The quilted,
glowing homes will get them through.

No school. D minus not A plus.
Some kids are waiting for the bus —
in darkness torch-beams swinging wide.

Out from the pubs on rainy days,
the vengeful village snitches gaze,
these barbers of dreams, teary-eyed.

MIDNIGHT MONOLOG

'How long will you be sowing that?
And, god, throw out those patches lest
you go bat blind on me... I could get
some paying work for us at last...

You weren't in the mountains with me.
And dancing.... I know, no dress to wear.
The frost had cooled us thoroughly...
We don't laugh. We don't cry. We stare.

I know a man who couldn't sleep
for fear appearances would slip –
an organ-grinder's monkey, dumb.

So, as for me, I know my place.
I know what's likely in my case:
all I will be I will become.'

RIGHT-THINKING WOMEN

The factory's non-stop noise and stink.
A peacock's tail of bright electrodes.
The blisters. The pinch of his two boots.
His collarbone's not-quite-healed chink

sends pain in torrents racing down
his back... Shamed by the swelter
of well-trained women welders.
He sees the load of work they've done

and knows he'll make no money here...
A siren goes off beside his ear.
The blast leaves them unfazed – it's noon.

Behind protective masks, all in leather,
like head-chefs, holding it together –
all they've burnt is their wooden spoons...

CHRISTMAS

The city flamed with brands of Christmas green –
the fires whipped round the yards day after day.
The doorbell. He went. She's standing there, no scene,
just: 'Since I'm here now, don't turn me away.'

Frost outside. In it a bare-limbed spruce.
'He threw you out?' The light shone at her touch:
her arms were covered with bruise after bruise.
She took a Sedolor; made up the couch.

Heard her asleep. He was awake all night.
War in the distance. Clatter of crutches. Unfurling
carpeting of bombs across Berlin.

On Unter den Linden she stuck out
in *feldgrau*. And it was *her* then at the gate.
Or was it just the darkness on the lookout?

A GRASS WIDOWER'S EVENING IN

Aches in his chest. Applies a compress.
And she's off to the ball – that dress! –
with their child. ('Rest! Take off the strain!
Tomorrow you'll be right as rain.')

He's wonderfully alone. It's been
hours since he took the medicine.
Lots take it to get through their lives,
especially life-sentenced wives.

He has his own plans. Unbedridden
he makes for where a bottle's hidden.
A P. T. coming from the zoo.

But suddenly it strikes him, No.
He has a better, older solution:
he reaches for the ageless Russians.

TV SCREEN

'Was I on TV? What a lark!
What was I like?' Strep throat, Brno
accent, an ELT friend, and now
some widower she met in a park.

In prison who slept where... (For her
all that was even just a game.)
The women: one after the other
those women got done all the same.

'My blood test's less than best. I'll pop
out tomorrow...' When will she stop?
Her head drop off in petrifaction?

The man who stood it and hadn't left her
and her prating – he must have loved her.
...Oh one fine day and nights no action.

ONE DAY

Stifling like 'Russia pre-reforms,'
aimless like people without families,
lame like a summer film release
tough like meeting daily norms...

like juddering, stuck in first gear, when
you start the car parked on a hill –
that's what the day was like. And still,
you know, the days go on. Again

the knout cracks round the circus ring,
again the clown's jokes, tired and spent,
again the loud applause's sound...

At every halt a circus tent,
the horses in them running, running,
however they want, round and round.

BANNERS OF KINGS

Discreet old hairdressers will soon
have done your hair for decades: wash
and trim and comb, sometimes a splash
of color. But one fine day they'll ruin

that gold, or maybe singe those locks.
One day their art will let them down.
Be ready for that. Tragedy stalks
in a grey mask, a blushing frown

that turns to smiles when bad breaks come.
Then cry at home – don't go to them,
the ones who loved that gold: though gutted,

they won't help you, themselves wrong-footed
the same way that most Europeans
can't tell Romani from Indians.

VILLAGE 1955

'Come. They're no longer out for blood.'
Years on… You're on the small train to
the village. Collective workers queue
to board, boots covered with farm mud.

A drunken uncle starts to shout,
'When will I join? Me? I choose my battles,'
and pulls the cork from one more bottle.
He downs it. Next morning, you go out

and walk into a different land.
A boy, wood whistle in his hand,
starts boasting, 'A Slovak taught me how

to carve it… The first shed there beyond.'
He doesn't know you've slept till now
and asks, 'Have they dealt with that cow?'

THE POET V. H. AT FIFTY

The world would soon be full of Sibyls
and prophesies of tar and feather
if human beings weren't able
to drive dread out into fair weather

and lead it through the city's streets
like a bearward brings a bear in thrall
even to God, who better treats
those who don't seek him out at all.

The lackeys have it in for those
who've realized how all this goes...
That pride can evil reach and prise

apart, that hard toil must be tholed,
he knows, this man, whose two hands hold
the very conscience of the skies.

September 16, 1955

CITY LIFE AND COUNTRY YOUTH

The apartments of the older Prague families
smell strange – perhaps the breeze
too rarely courses through the rooms and these,
their dusty bibelots, doze on with ease.

In the Czech Highlands, over its hills,
we never could outstep our shadows, still
just seventeen or so, testing our will
on Old Slavonic dictionaries and drills.

Sunday-less years of love. So daunted,
these boys without the first idea
what women actually wanted.

Now sober and now drunk, and thus
up to our necks in feelings… History
knows this and lives in style off us.

For Dr. Mirko Zeman

A GRACEFUL LITTLE BEAR

Night. The Karlovy Vary express
more like a boxcar on the rails.
And then police raids – three no less
and not once did they… Routine drills…

Bags in the aisle. He saw her there
straight off, mousy, drenched to the skin.
Darkness behind her. Her frazzled air.
A velvet seat for two! Squeezed in…

Wet gardens. Hoses uncoiling.
The perspiration from hot dogs.
And how she lost her shoes in spring,

in mud time. And those gift catalogs…
her brother's wedding... When she was leaving,
he helped her off the train? Not even.

A ZOOT SUITER'S HISTORY
OF THE BEGINNING OF THE END

'…they started making coffins cozy
for yes-man fuck-ups in the Party.
Old songs now didn't seem so hearty.
Cravats bored them – too blowzy-rosy…

Bookmakers were finished. The lads
were after only cash and power.
Evenings, they'd put pipes and rads
in large flats split in three or four…

And those who *always* went scot-free,
no matter what, were in the pokey.
The super'd whisper to a comrade…

Some dodgy army anecdotes…
And suddenly they only thing they had
the measure of was their own coats…'

SHORT CIRCUIT

Еще обиду тянет с блюдца
Невыспавшееся дитя,
А мне уж не на кого дуться,
И я один на всех путях.
Osip Mandelstam

The parquets spread through parks. And those
bright lanterns! Then the power goes.
A sea of darkness that would steal
the charge from an electric eel.

And all those girls are now corralled
by carnival enchantment.
...A different girl here tightly held
in this black night, as in a tent.

And there is no other now
except that time... And you want to know?
Not yours. Not theirs. Nobody's.

I'm whose I'm not, as I am known,
when on all roads there blows a breeze,
on those same roads I walk alone.

PART III

MEMORY'S THREE MOVEMENTS

A town with two industrial plants,
a pond for casting lines into,
and out beyond the graveyard's fence
some woods that lie in wait for you…

Skulls studded in the church's wall,
a grave in clay, the bible sold,
and who knows where's the bed at all
she couldn't sleep in, tossed and rolled…

On Saturday, the dusk calls up
the football players from the pub;
and Sunday knows the push and pull

of silence, as lovers go in pairs
into spring woodlands, which are full
of sleepy, shaded hunters' lairs.

TECHNICAL PROGRESS

You see it briefly, that bewilderment
in older people, baffled by hindrance,
confused as they try leaving through an entrance –
the look in their eyes: 'You, what do you want?'

The world constrains them like a bathyscaph,
as they, submersed, try on style after style
(each one, at least once, all the rage a while),
poised and ready to break the warp and woof.

The elevators and the planes as yet
have not relieved them of their earthly weight.
Their death will solve the issue well before

the summer cottages are turned into
the backdrop for a drama, wholly new
– as fitting in their way as Elsinore.

A CHILD GIVES A RUNNING COMMENTARY
ON THE SECOND HALF

She does the diapers, breastfeeds, nuzzles –
the nail ingrown in the age.
You'd like to sleep out of the puzzle
of your own self, out of that cage.

A child is scared of animals –
he wakes, he wails, and then he yawns.
You only can't find warmth, but females,
mothers, they know where: with sons.

Your only goal 'the ball in net.'
Write where you want of 'leagues upset.'
Like a coach whose club is closed and barred…

And don't be riled by yellow cards.
It's women and not freedom who
give birth to children. This you knew?

HERE SHOULD BLOSSOM

...the young girl
no more than a child...
that was before she turned whore...
William Carlos Williams

Love story laced with naphthalene,
threatening that it would set off
– like the seeping gas... did Jana mean... –
a swirl of slander and what-if.

Even the sun rose that day... printed!
Columbus aired the mothers' earth
after the discus – gold it glinted –
that Olga threw for all she's worth.

The galley proofs flew from my heels
when they were married in newsreels.
The deadline's heat... The scorching rays

(lemons and oranges, nights and days)
but cooled then in the girls' wet hair
done shooting hoops in the night air.

For Josef Škvorecký

A BORROWED BOOK

'You'll find no kittens in Chagall —
he's thatched roofs and what you'd guess is a
white horse over frozen forests and all
the dark shamashes of Odessa...'

A winged head then came drifting down
and kissed another head — clearest
of proofs that this head is the one —
of all the other heads the dearest.

'...love's pulse, beneath which you're a whirl
of horses racing. My longing spurned
and pitied by you — was it grotesque?

That night still lasts, but now she's turned
her back to me, like that bared girl
from childhood towns, *Nude over Vitebsk*...'

For Věra Linhartová

FOR KAREL ČERNÝ

A coarseness here that hardly brushes
this heaven with no rose retouches.
Our heaven seen from the viewpoint
of two half-pints, of two half-pints.

Such anger: that even true blue dreams
still play out as our fortune deems.
Not vengeance, but he scorned the wreck
of an age with no Tarpeian Rock.

Hounded out of his own skin
and mad for costume changes, he'd show
a pair of girlish fists to spar

and hate: he saw a man (A MAN!)
with happy talismans sail far
across the River Styx's flow.

♀

The invite scares you. A faded mop
for hair, and teeth with stains and spots.
And the heart quickly cools and sets
like dripping taken off the hob.

Your long life had a shorter sortie
within it, when the leaves turned green
and everything blossomed between
the ages of thirteen and forty.

So what to do? Invite neighbors
and friends, read books, and gradually feel
the blood in your veins slowing down,

brew up some tea and have your meal.
You won't have any further cares
when your times of the month are done.

FOR A LIVING WOMAN

Where did she go? She's where nowadays?
If only she'd gone! Still she passes
into long rooms of canvasses
viewed through a strong painkillers' haze.

Maybe she swapped the thrust and parry
for boredom in the years succeeding.
Maybe after she'd miscarried
she got up quickly, bleeding...

Maybe she mocked up storyboards:
Lovers, 1950s (in their hordes).
She'd tell all-comers who she had.

No, settling down was not for her.
I'd say she cuts scenes, doesn't add.
And there has never been another.

'YEARS OF YOUTH'

The pork numb in vast concrete halls.
Mild satire worse than none at all.
'Don't steal my heart, my heart that ails!'
And all in jail. And all in jail.

Trials like black masses televised.
Progress? Our cat had had enough.
We had a five-year plan for love,
but it was never realized.

Horizon of walls, all with ears.
The weevil worked good souls to tears.
Truths hard to swallow through the years...

The sparrows hidden in cherry trees...
Recall the plays and penalties!
Recall the days... What came of these!

42 NA POŘÍČÍ STREET

Now other lovers breathe that air.
The flat's not winter's, it's July's.
Maybe your daughter's there somewhere.
The new bars full of new barflies.

Don't think, though, you won't raise a spark
from those whose breaths now heave and wheeze.
There old phone numbers maybe work
undialled in out-of-date directories.

There David, deaf, clutches a harp.
There at the movies blind men stare.
There time turned its dial brusque and sharp
down on our sojourn's ambient noises.

And after us a statue of voices.
And after us a statue of air.

THIRTY

The ball I threw while playing in the park
Has not yet touched the ground...
Dylan Thomas

We'll never be as happy as those times. . .
Yes and? Who cares they won't repeat?
What's to be done with our old rhymes?
We'll grind them into sausage meat.

What's to be done with our old debts?
They'll turn into fa la la la.
Will they come for them? Drop their threats?
They'll cry like some Ophelia.

Or will we sit there always, no sound
but clinking cups, hiccups, a belch or bark,
new needles sunk into old wounds,

content on days that small gifts mark?
*...The ball thrown high while playing in the park
Has not yet touched the ground...*

POETS, PROPHETS, ETC.

They prophesied just fine, like scripture,
as though uplifted by the stars.
And their obsessive holy rapture
filled shelves in secondhand bookstores.

And nights, they leaned into the paper
and heard: 'I block your way. I lie.'
(The lines made it a striped tapir.)
'You'll sink. You'll scream. And then you'll die.

Give up...' (observe a top's tight threads
transform two breasts into pike heads).
Glass tiles in putty reassured

them how to get out. So it proved.
First light... Into the morning's azure
the specter of great libraries hoved.

JEALOUSY

To know she carries letters toward
that garish postbox as in the past.
That she has others now, who've scored
their goals in those long-open posts.

That she'll shake off the awful lashings
of faux pas (boredom kept at bay).
That she'll earn even from her passions
(that they're not serious anyway).

To know ahead when and which tone
and for whom she'll take on the phone.
To know the knife she'll use on you

straight in your back, the words, the glove...
It's easy to be cruel in love –
withholding it will do.

RITUAL

In the hour like yellow ivory,
when the razor draws bright red on gray.
When passion drops its livery
in Prague's four-four time at cockcrow.

When walking to the door there come
in leather coats two morning guests.
When love at last stops playing dumb —
it just distracts from death's behest.

When rounded limbs forget their hurry
and suddenly are freed of worry.
When faithfulness, bereft of color,

stares like an anchorite in high
apartments, overheated, dry,
where the only water soaks a collar...

LEAVE

And I say leave, oh leave,
and be free of the scribbled pages.
Jiří Valja

Going through the motions on the pitch.
Played out. We've kicked so long for touch
that Time offsets this not so much
in heresy but more in kitsch.

Freight cars of words go up in flames
en route and under these conditions
we're seen as typos, still the same
in even third and fourth editions.

Who knew the wounds they didn't dress
would be OK! The bloodiest mess
were those they bandaged neat and trim –
those wounds would turn the world from him.

Death to the mortal! Worse still, his welts
so thick, death in a stranger's pelt.

TOWERBLOCK ESTATE

The windows twist round creeping vines.
Free of others? Here's hoping, daily.
New solitude (and nerves – new signs).
What was withheld is now flogged gaily.

The verdant leaves torn by despair
that sees all here, unvarying.
Gaze upward? In the dentist's chair
perhaps – the ceiling endless, boring.

Cars revving, saunas, body wounds,
the evenings spent with 'our old friends.'
Make-up along the TV's edge.

Payments, taxes, policies lapsed,
lost in the endless rows, collapsed
in on oneself, into old age.

BLACK MORNING MEMORY

Apartment. He'd leave it as night sank
in silence toward the morning
to a future featureless and blank,
from a past of voodoo warnings,

when the moon hung on a parachute
of silken clouds the sky outspread,
when even bars stood closed and mute
after the football herds had fled...

Even if he went hurrying back
and combed the trash, bag after bag,
today it all would be a blur:

those diaries (long lost in the scrim) –
just some... 'he loved her'...
just some... 'she him'...

PART IV

DEMONS

Now only grass croons of the future,
alarm clocks strewn across it, thrown
from windows. Beneath it bones – foot to
spine – and the sweetest months we've known.

And they'll stop eating meat once more,
count calories and run up flags.
Today's blood, like the day before

yesterday's juts from hands like jags.
Tomorrow: top-secret curtains drawn
to chasten truth. SO BRIEFLY BARED.
Again, they'll march us up and down,
to oaths I never came to swear.

Upon my life, the tracks have vanished,
We've lost our way, what shall we do?
It must be a demon's leading us
This way and that around the fields.

Prague, August 25, 1968

71

SEASON TICKET

Death comes before the 'Finally!' –
mid-speech, before they loose the sash.
It's paid up front and, miserly,
it wants full value for its cash.

Not 'finally!' – death comes before.
Before the auditorium's dark.
For those who spit on it, and more.
For those who feel for it a spark
of love, though who could know the score,
so loudly they say life's a lark.

Death always sits in the first rows.
Oblivious to power and spin.
For us it has a text in prose
it wants rhymed with the *mise-en-scène*.

March 18, 1977

AUBADE

'Wake up, come on, wake up! Life's waiting.
The kettle's boiled. There's sugar here.
Or will I send him off? Rain skating
down the glass and penetrating
your very eyelids, tear on tear.

It's cartoon bright out. Sunrays ring us
as they do clichéd couples sometimes.
It's calling us. It wants to swing us.
We're doves. It dives for us to fling us
out of the night that teems with crimes...'

'This light... won't we be swallowed by it?
Your poems. Me too, for all my beauty.
And dead in it, we will be quiet,
but still rise early. That's our duty.'

July 3, 1977

GOLDEN SCALP

He lost his paddle at the first weir,
and sank his love, his boat, his home.
Where were you? Doing laundry here
and serving builders spuds and ham.

He tipped an urn and fed the heart
to birds, to their chirping amazement.
Where were you? Sweeping the chickens' yard
beside the fuchsia and white casement.

He waited for what? Tear-bleached photos?
The nothing after puberty?
Where were you? Driving our flash motor
to rile the residents' committee.

He closed those doors only to skelp
a scalp – only your golden scalp.

July 3, 1977

SCHOOLMATES

What's childhood got to do with me?
Where are they? *Are* they? Some might be

pumping gas, or making headway
with their careers… Like a display
of next year's urns. Their existence
is best left in the darkened distance.
That flesh orphaned by love's first flush
is still for me that lovely flesh,
that witnessed me… Girls sweeter than
all others, brisk as rataplan –
their dads like lightning off the plate…

Oh it was all a laugh, and itching
to get out, we're kept back for mitching,
and we'll be home for dinner late.

September 14, 1977

OFFERTORY AFFAIR

The next dead person looks OK.
In decent fettle at first glance.
The back a bit hunched. The gaze grey.
He looks at everything askance.

And then he's all on for a beer.
'And bring the blonde one – she looked great.'
Big laughs. Some general good cheer.
A few jokes five years out of date.

Red-letter love, oh I know you:
your coat has hung in many rooms;
and your path leads between the tombs.

Better than one alone, us two.
Until I put my head into
the stove for you… and gulp the fumes.

i.m. Jiří Pištora
November 9, 1977

VANITY

I carted junk across the bridges.
I chopped a brolly up for fuel.
Slept in manure. Rotted in ditches.
Oh I was shaking like a fool
because of love's brutal surprises
(a flyblown riddle she'd contrived).
I envied Botvinnik his prizes.
Enamelled old pots. And survived
the cheeky pup rejecting me.
I gargled blood and horehound tea.
I didn't play the priest with sheep.
When politicians raged I'd sleep.
I tapped on walls to those stuffed there,
before I turned my gaze elsewhere.

December 18, 1977

Goe, and catche a falling starre...
Tell me, where all past yeares are...
John Donne

THAT ONE, THAT I

And then the world gave him a drubbing.
Might kill him yet. One of the crew
back then, before he started blubbing.
Fratello. He was one we knew.
Then his tone changed. Was night so dark it
made him stick out like a target.

My night. Someone else's stars.
Beneath the wig, a dust that stirs.
And someone else's specs and teeth
through which the muffled festivals breathe.
An elf sings in the flask of night;
a worm in mud sends him pure spite.
And worm rage and elf song I'll save
to deck my coffin in the grave.

January 2, 1978

PIGEONS

Grey waves that yawl and tack
about the sky, these float,
these pigeons coming back
to darkness in the dovecote.

Life's brief, and we are raced
and briskly roiled about,
all of us in the rest,
a gift for them, held out,

a flurry of wings and names
in gold wood fire, which seems
a fete in window frames

only, from far away —
distant songs, distant dreams,
far off a pigeon grey.

March 5, 1978

Жизнъ ведъ тоже толъко миг,
Толъко растворенъе
Нас самих во всех других
Как бы им в даренъе.
Boris Pasternak

SUMMER'S END

The first set only, a bit of fight.
The playboy cheated by a sleight.
They ruined the summer on that Wednesday,
a ball that skewed when it hit clay.
Play not restarted, despite the call –
the cage was just about to fall.

For summer and for the Olympics,
for our high hopes on stilts, the fix
was in: the streets on that warm morning
rang with our brothers' gentle warning.

That summer, darkness fell forever,
its fun a total killer.
There's only grey the whole world over –
it fills in every color.

For Ivan Wernisch
March 5, 1978

ENCYCLOPEDIA ENTRY

The past's a tin-can filled with ash.
The past's a sleeping bag with fleas.
For friends who felt the lash and backlash,
on whom they've thrown away the keys.

The past's great towns seen from a train,
no piggin poked with many mickles.
The past is smog, grey vats of brine
we swim through like a shoal of pickles.

It's crabs strung into necklace art,
a room where samba instrumentals
set undertakers dancing, a mart
where lullabies are swapped for lentils.

Hide-and-Seek we played with it,
but it played with us Counting Out.

April 7, 1978

TABLOID READER

'Beat stepson so hard in a fight
though he kept crying: "Mommy! Mommy!"'
'A widow, healthy, and still fit,
would like to – *die?* – with car and hobby.'

'...the key was hooked and then pulled smartly
beneath the door...' '...steaks grilled, beers cold
and all laid on, till officers called...
broke up the good-for-nothings' party.'

'...despite the watch a girl by far
at hatcheck at the Rio Bar...'
'Uncle Trumbald back from rehab –

a false alarm, he's feeling fab!'
'After the Gala Travesties
brought in toward morning without testes!'

For Josef Brukner
May 28, 1983

UNGALLANT CONVERSATION

'No, I don't know him… A son? A friend?'
Oh leave… 'an admirer… penned
some poems?' …*Blind test and this gallant
was found as you, listless, attend
the rise of fresh, aspiring talent…*

'My mom told me you knew each other…'
Hmm, knew… Five years I slept with her.

'…thing is, they're good, for all their faults,
if you avoid Fellini schmaltz…'
'Yep, carp will always lay their roe
even in acid.' The schmo

then cries: 'Calls for a beer, I'd say!
But after you…' *I couldn't put it more
precisely: my prick passed through that way
before, not after you. Before.*

May 30, 1983

ADAPTED FROM THE AUTHOR'S NOTES

Passages from foreign texts enter poems as they were in the original: fragments heard, read or remembered; evidently also from a distaste towards the conventions referred to as pure poetic speech. The epigraphs below the poems are of different kinds: in some cases to indicate that the paraphrase or quote is used in the lines of the poem itself; elsewhere they connect to the matter of the poem or to a literary analogy. The following notes are provided at the request of the editors. – JZ

[Notes that translate English texts have been omitted. In the note to 'Banners of the Kings,' I give JZ's translation, even though it is erroneous, as it is an interesting error. The correction follows in brackets. – JQ]

'Summer 1944' – *Sterbe wohl, Erika* (Die happily, Erika). Adjusted words of the song of Hitler's troops, 'Lebe wohl, Erika' (Live happily, Erika).

'Splendid Isolation Destroyed' – the title is given in English in the Czech original.

'Khlestakov Visits the Harvest Home, Summer 1945' – *Lieber Heini!* is 'Dear Hal!'

'Evenings Trains' – Путъ далек лежит (The journey is long). From an old Russian song 'Ямщик' (The coachman), which the Red Army Choir often sang in Czechoslovakia in 1945.

'Decembrists' – Lafite and Veuve-Clicquot: French wines. Alexander Pushkin mentions them in *Eugene Onegin*, the fragment of the tenth chapter.

'Psalm': A paraphrase of Psalm 124: Anima nostra sicut passer erepta est de laqueo venantium (Our soul is escaped as a bird out of the snare of the fowlers…)

'Banners of the Kings' – remembered from a schoolbook: *Vexilla regis prodeunt inferni* (forth go the banners of the king of hell). [JZ misremembered this and gave here the Czech translation: 'The banners of the kings approach.']

'Short Circuit – *Еще обиду тянет*… (The child who has not slept well / still sucks his indignation from a saucer, / but I have no one to blame, and wherever I go I'm alone. From Osip Mandelstam's poem, 'Oh, how we love to play the hypocrite,' here in Elizabeth and Richard McKane's translation.

'Here Should Blossom' – From Book V of *Paterson*, by William Carlos Williams.

'A Borrowed Book' – *Nude over Vitebsk*, the painting by Marc Chagall.

'Leave' – '*And I say leave, oh leave…*' from Jiří Valja's poem, 'Candor,' published in the *Spring Poetry Almanac 1940*.

ZÁBRANA OVERHEARD

Justin Quinn

1

W. B. Yeats was surely wrong when he wrote that 'we make out of the quarrel with others, rhetoric, but of the quarrel with ourselves, poetry.'[1] This suggests that poetry, in its essence, has no public dimension, that the realms of politics, of community, of shared experiences more generally, don't belong in the genre, which is better suited to expressions of the inner spirit. Of course, the first place to look for evidence that Yeats was wrong is in his own poetry. Many of his poems resonated, and still resonate, in public forums, while others that talk of love and of spirit make some fine rhetorical moves. Still, the dictum can't quite be discounted, as it suggests that poetry can somehow reach deeper into the spirit than any other literary genre.

We encounter some of these paradoxes in the poetry of Jan Zábrana (1931–1984), above all in his 1968 collection, *The Lesser Histories* (in Czech, *Stránky z deníku*, which can be literally translated as *Pages from a Diary*). He began writing many of these sonnets in the 1950s, a calamitous decade in Czechoslovakia's history, when political repression had perverted public poetry, turning it into tinkling rhymes by wide-eyed ideologists who were infatuated by mass murderers. In contrast, Zábrana in his poetry seems, at times, to be talking to himself. He rejects *tout court* a wider audience, choosing mostly to write of himself and his own experience in the second- or third-person singular. He frequently addresses disappointments in love or in himself. In these poems we can never quite escape public events, however. We have an acute sense that the snatches of conversation and song that the poet hears (and overhears) resonate in that larger arena, but Zábrana, although tempted throughout his life, would never raise his voice enough to fill that space.

---

[1] W. B. Yeats, *Later Essays*, ed. William H. O'Donnell (New York: Scribner's, 1994), epub, 26.

2

In summer 1982, two years before his death, Zábrana reflected on his life and career. He had spent the previous three decades working as a professional translator of mostly detective stories, poetry, and novels, working long days for uncertain honorariums. As his stature as a translator rose, he had some leeway in the choice of work, but the daily grind was unremitting. Many passages in his diaries document this tedium, and, increasingly in the 1970s, the other central dilemma of his life:

> Why should I worry about the way my life looks – about the fact that, aside from work, it no longer resembles a life in any way? After all, it isn't my life. The life I considered my own ended in November 1949. Would anyone believe me if I told them that November 1949 is more vivid, more burning, more present for me – even at this very moment – than is July 1982, when I'm writing these words? And that, if I'm not dying from my old wounds, it's only because I'm not actually alive? Would anyone believe me if I told them that the pain inside me has only been growing more intense with time, that a thirty-three-year-old pain is, for me, right now, worse and more unbearable than it was thirty-three years ago? It's two-thirty a.m. I woke up and turned on the light and I'm writing in this notebook. I woke up with a feeling of horror, pain, and despair over what happened thirty-three years ago. And my mother, whom they arrested and carried off at five in the morning, hasn't been alive for more than eight years. But the despair of that morning persists. It woke me on this stifling Saturday night.[2]

When World War II ended in May 1945, another struggle began that would decide the political terrain of Europe during the next four decades. The USSR began to bring states into its sphere of influence, and Russian emissaries cooperated with local Communist parties to expand Soviet influence. Disgusted by Nazism and mindful of the endemic poverty that preceded

---

[2] Jan Zábrana, *Celý život* (Prague: Torst, 2001), 982. The translation here, and all subsequent translations from this source, are by Jonathan Bolton. His selection and translation of Zábrana's diaries, under the title *All My Life*, is in progress.

the war, many Europeans embraced communism. By the beginning of 1948, it was still unclear which side of the Iron Curtain Czechoslovakia would find itself on. Both within and without the country, many hoped that it would be possible to find a third way through the Cold War. But in February, the Czechoslovak Communists staged a putsch, and those hopes died.

Zábrana was born in the village of Herálec in the Czech Highlands, and grew up in the larger town of Humpolec. In many respects, his parents represented the flower of Czechoslovak society. Both were active members in one of the country's social democratic parties and teachers who followed and helped instigate education reforms in the country. Zábrana's mother, Jiřina, through her journalism and lecturing, was the more prominent of the two. She associated with luminaries such as Františka Plamínková, the leading feminist of the day (executed by the Nazis in 1945), and Milada Horáková, the social democrat and member of Parliament (later executed by the Communist regime after a show trial in 1950). Zábrana's parents also represented the best of the First Republic, that is, Czechoslovakia in the period 1918–1938, which was liberal, democratic, reformist, and nationalist (in a complex way as the country contained many nations); indeed, Zábrana's mother was in contact on several occasions with Czechoslovakia's founder, Tomáš Garrigue Masaryk. In 1979, Zábrana sighed in his diaries thus:

> Oh, the First Republic… Amidst the despair of all these quickly passing years, I see ever more clearly that just one happiness remains to me: at least I experienced those seven childhood years in the First Republic, was still able to feel its air, that unsurpassable and singular atmosphere of freedom… The war was horrifying, but compared to what came in the 1950s, it had one basic advantage: everyone understood it as an interruption, at the end of which was waiting some reconnection with the First Republic. Today, the two and a half years from May 1945 to February 1948 seem to me like a short-lived continuation of what existed in this country before the war – the same feeling of happiness…[3]

---

3   Zábrana, *Celý život*, 705.

He shared this feeling with many Czechs, for whom the First Republic represented the halcyon days of the country's history, especially when viewed from the 1970s and '80s.

Then, on November 8, 1949, agents of Czechoslovak State Security arrested Jiřina Zábranová at the family home in the early hours of the morning. In May of the following year, she was condemned to eighteen years imprisonment for high treason and espionage. Zábrana's father Emanuel had to retrain as a painter of porcelain in a workshop 50 kilometers from the family home. In October 1951, however, Emanuel was also arrested and condemned to ten years. (The sentences of both parents were commuted in 1960, though their convictions were not overturned.) Zábrana applied to the Faculty of Arts of Charles University in Prague in 1950 to study languages, but was turned down for political reasons. He moved to Prague anyway, where he studied theology for a few semesters and then worked in the Tatra Smíchov factory, spending most weekends during the decade making long journeys across the country to visit his parents in different prisons.

In 1976, Zábrana wrote that 'the difference between the first and second half of life – taken subjectively, that is, based on how we feel – lies above all in one thing: in the first half of life, you're on the side of the beautiful and the promising, while in the second half, you're on the side of those who are ugly and washed-up.'[4] But across this personal divide, another deeper cut was made into the nation as a whole, intensifying Zábrana's later feeling of alienation from his younger self. This is what lies behind the diary entry of 1974: 'To all those who keep asking me to do things for them, I sometimes feel like saying: "But I'm dead. I died long ago. Why do you keep treating me as if I were one of the living?"'[5]

---

[4] Zábrana, Celý život, 436.
[5] Zábrana, Celý život, 311.

3

So, by his own account, from 1949 to 1984, Zábrana was a dead man walking. He had no public life: he never spoke out, not even after the Warsaw Pact invasion of Czechoslovakia in August 1968. Often, in his diaries, he explodes that he has a mind to tell X or Y what he really thinks, but this soon subsides, as he admits to himself that he will never do it. Unlike Václav Havel, his close friend from the 1950s, he was not a vocal opponent of the regime; and unlike the internationally known Czech poet Miroslav Holub (whom Zábrana disliked), neither did he enjoy the privileges of keeping quiet (such as travel and official tolerance of foreign publication). He was aware of his situation and his abilities to respond to it:

> This is how the era toys with me. I am able to say no, but not very loudly. I'm not afraid of death, but I wouldn't be able to summon it myself. I'm not capable of any deed. I feel like everything inside me is agitated, trembling, in pain.... And so I am unbound but broken, uncertain, unsatisfied, laughable in my own eyes, bound up in my mask of arrogant aloofness. I find it oppressive. In normal times, I would have a hard time stepping out of it, but now, when the burden would be doubled, I'm just not capable. I wouldn't do it. My will simply couldn't take it.[6]

Yet, we may also turn Zábrana's statement upside down and declare that in fact his life began in 1949. In many respects, as his diaries of the time attest, he was already politically mature, capable of penetrating analyses of the situation in Czechoslovakia, as well as in Europe (he wrote the passage above at the age of seventeen). During the early 1950s in Prague, he came into contact with a wide range of future important cultural figures such Bohumil Hrabal, Věra Linhartová, Jiří Kolář, Josef Škvorecký, and Havel, who would become President in 1989. Some of these were friends, Škvorecký, above all. This pleiad would serve as a surrogate college, providing a superior education to that offered by Charles University, which had been whipped into

---

[6]   Zábrana, Celý život, 83.

ideological line after 1948. He also applied to the Translators' Association and was accepted. In practical terms, this meant that he was freed from the obligation to seek other employment and could work from home. He subsequently became one of the top translators of his generation. In 1997, the writer Patrick Ouředník remarked that 'a translator of Zábrana's stature appears once every fifty or hundred years in any given language.'[7] This expresses a widely held opinion. In spring 1955, he had an important love affair. In 1963, he married Marie Leskovjanová; a year later, their daughter, Eva, was born. Over the next twenty years, he would write thousands of pages of diaries, translate an impressive number of works from English and Russian, and publish three collections of poems, one in 1965, and two in 1968, one of which was *The Lesser Histories*.

4

1968: he could not have chosen a worse year to publish the collection. On the night of the 20 to 21 August, Warsaw Pact forces invaded Czechoslovakia and the remaining sixteen years of Zábrana's life were spent under a regime that was reasserting ideological control of Czechoslovakia. In the early 1960s, he moved with his wife Marie, to a towerblock estate in the new Prague suburb of Malešice, still by his own account a dead man living. From there, he continued translating and writing long diary entries. He also added a fourth section to *The Lesser Histories* (the original publication ended with the poem 'Black Morning Memory'). This final section opens with 'Demons,' written three days after the Warsaw Pact invasion. These poems added darker notes of bitterness and betrayal, the bleakest of which is perhaps 'Ungallant Conversation.' But they are also interleaved by poems like 'Summer's End,' 'Pigeons,' and 'Tabloid Reader,' which bring to perfec-

---

[7] Patrik Ouředník, "Prezydent, nebo Krokadýl? Ke sporu o autorství jednoho překladu," *Kritická příloha Revolver Revue* 7 (1997): 117. Also available at https://www.nllg.eu/spip .php?article539.

tion Zábrana's disinterested, meticulous observation of the world. There are even moments of humor ('Offertory Affair'), as Zábrana considers the series of friends he confronts in their coffins: 'The next dead person looks OK.' There is also the pathos of 'Schoolmates,' which wonders where these people are now; he loops their later, unknown lives back to child-hood, in the last line, as he imagines their dinner waiting for them, while they roam the world, and the afterlife.

From his apartment, he also had a clear view of all the people who were happy to be housed at last. Like many European countries on both sides of the Iron Curtain, Czechoslovakia was frenetically building for new urban populations. In Sweden, for instance, this was called the *Miljonprogrammet*, or Million Program; in France, there was the push to build *Habitation à Loyer Modéré* (housing at moderate rent). He viewed these neighbors with a jaundiced eye:

> You can see quite a distance from the eighth floor of our building – in all directions. You see people, families, who couldn't exist without a car. It fills up their mornings, afternoons, and evenings. They're always driving off somewhere, driving back from somewhere, washing their cars – it's clear that they fall asleep thinking about them, wake up thinking about them. As if they had been born to ride in cars. Outside their cars, they lead a completely gray existence, even in their own eyes, you can tell from the expression on their faces – they only light up when they sit behind the wheel.[8]

This is the view of a man born in the country who never really settled in the new urban environment of the capital. It could have been written in Swe-den or France. Such a feeling of *anomie* pervades poems like 'Towerblock Estate,' 'Black Morning Memory,' and 'Demons.' He was alienated from his life and his country by communism; he was also alienated from the twen-tieth century.

---

[8] Zábrana, *Celý život*, 279.

If Zábrana felt exiled from the life and values promised by his upbringing (and this occasionally precipitates an ironic tone toward the era of the First Republic), he also rails against what might be best figured as the ceiling seen from the dentist's chair in the new socialist urban environment ('Tower-block Estate'). The first line of '"Years of Youth"' refers to 'the pork numb in vast concrete halls,' and this image structures his wide ranging consideration of the Czechoslovak Socialist Republic: just as the pig carcasses hang in cold abattoirs, so, too, do Czechoslovak citizens inhabit the new Socialist towerblock estates.

In their hostile outlook on modern life, The Lesser Histories and the diaries at times resemble Theodor Adorno's Minima Moralia: Reflections on a Damaged Life (1951). The German philosopher, exiled to Los Angeles during World War II, had an analogous deep, hurt sense that he had been cheated of life as it should be, as though European and US culture more generally had been perverted. Every tiny facet of the modern world is indicted – marriage, artworks, the discovery of dinosaurs, and even casual gestures. all are symptoms of a damaged epoch. Culture itself is just the circulation of lies, and 'that culture so far has failed is no justification for furthering its failure, by strewing the store of good flour on the spilt beer like the girl in the fairy-tale.'[9] Such a feeling of pervasive malaise is common in both men's work. Just as Zábrana sees cultural exchange in Communist Czechoslovakia as distorted by totalitarianism, so Adorno sees the relationship between culture and capitalism, immediately from Los Angeles, where he was living at the time of writing, but also Europe, as perverted from its earlier promise by capitalist exchange. Likewise, both men continued to work either for or in organizations that were implicated in the systems that their writings deplored – Zábrana as part of the Communist 'culture industry' of Czechoslovak literary publishers, and Adorno as a lec-

---

[9] Theodor W. Adorno, Minima Moralia: Reflections on a Damaged Life, trans. E. F. N. Jephcott (London: Verso, 2005), epub. Part 1, 'Baby with the Bath Water.'

turer and administrator in a tertiary-level educational institution. Both also despised the aspects of social amelioration that could be seen both in the US and throughout Europe in the postwar period, as they believed that it flattened complex articulations of cultural tradition, reducing them to economic exchange (again, whether part of capitalism or communism), much in the manner that Le Corbusier wished to raze centuries-old accretions of architecture in cities and replace them with ranks of towerblocks on squat stilts, surrounded by highways. To repeat: Adorno lived in a democracy, whereas Zábrana lived under a Communist regime. That difference, though important, should not occlude continuities. Central to both of their works was the vilification of an epoch that had created what Adorno's Frankfurt School colleague, Herbert Marcuse, labelled, 'one-dimensional man.'

5

During his life, Zábrana experienced two severe crackdowns, the first in the wake of the putsch in 1948, and the second after the Warsaw Pact invasion of 1968. Later in the 1970s, as the regime loosened ever so slightly, even some of Zábrana's friends and acquaintances began to speculate about adjusting their own careful distance from the state administration. Apparatchiks also began to admit publicly that mistakes had been made, and lessons learned. Zábrana was unconvinced. On such occasions (after a meeting, or after hearing a pronouncement on the radio), he would recite a long and thorough litany of communism's offenses. In his view, they committed their worst crimes in the early years of the regime, and that guilt would never be erased or mitigated by any compromises or apologies. And variations on one idea repeat throughout the diaries, always presented as irrefutable and final proof of their guilt: they were capable of executing women.[10]

There are several dead women in *The Lesser Histories* ('Dead Girl Remembered,' 'For a Dead Girl,' not one 'Witch Burning,' but two). The

---

[10]   Zábrana, *Celý život*, 172, 187, 194–5, 227, 407, 759, 821, 985.

witches are likely references to the victims of communism. Although only one woman, Milada Horáková, was executed, her death came to symbolize all the women who suffered violence at the hands of the Communists. In those witch-burning poems the accusation is drowned by Zábrana's sense of guilt that he let this happen. (As one diary entry notes: 'Am I supposed to spend my whole life agonizing over the memory of how they skewered you on a roasting spit? Nothing seemed more important – then. Nothing seems less interesting – now.'[11]) The other cases seem, at least in part, expressions of voyeuristic lyricism, reworkings of the old male theme of a young woman's death, with its mixture of eros and loss. They are also opportunities to survey the era's collective violence, some of it misogynistic ('Dead Girl Remembered'), and elsewhere to glimpse the whole world from outside (as at the end of 'For a Dead Girl'). One or two other poems express a listless suspicion of or cynicism toward women (for instance, 'Sublet,' 'A Sentimental Journey,' 'Midnight Monolog'). 'Jealousy' in particular brims with animosity and disdain; it is most likely about a woman with whom he had an intense affair in his early Prague days, and who he discovered was cheating on him.

There is a forceful sexual edge to most of this, which cannot always be corralled in the sphere of the personal, but is interwoven with the seething political violence of his lifetime (they hanged women). Communism proclaimed itself enlightened and progressive on the question of gender, and did indeed bring about some improvements. So, the flipside of Zábrana's representations of women above was his detailed sardonic view of the Communist regime's ideal female. One diary entry quotes a radio program: "'…the women at Strahov Stadium – this is a collective expression of the happiness of individually happy Czechoslovak women…" Zábrana carefully notes the date and even time of the broadcast (June 9, 1975, 11:25am –

---

11   Zábrana, *Celý život*, 845.

99

one more entry in the book of evidence he is compiling).[12] And in 1981, he reports to his diary that Prague is hosting another Congress of Women. The headline in *Rudé právo*, the Party newspaper, runs: 'Uniting Women in the Struggle for Peace and against the Threat of Nuclear War…' Zábrana comments that 'when I saw this, I realized it was a belated but cogent rejoinder (the first two words, at least) to a poem I wrote more than a quarter of a century ago:

> …*there still are crowds*
> of solitary women.
>
> What's important is
> that they never unite.[13]

(Again, for the book of evidence, Zábrana gives the page number and title of his own collection.) A feminist of our time might see this as an expression of the wish to keep women separate and governable by men, as objects of male desire. Indeed, there are many passages that mull over the sexual attractions of women, but this may be an anachronistic reading. Communists did not allow citizens to form associations outside official structures, and that included any feminist organization. Some of these ideas come together in 'Right-thinking Women,' about his Stakhanovite fellow female factory workers in his early Prague days at Tatra Smíchov. No passage in the diaries expresses hostility toward the feminism of his mother's circle. But that earlier feminism of the First Republic was co-opted and emptied of much meaning by the Communist regime. So, if we are to read Zábrana as anti-feminist, we must also acknowledge that the only possible version of feminism that was active in his adult life was organized and promoted by a repressive regime.

---

12   Zábrana, *Celý život*, 377.
13   Zábrana, *Celý život*, 847.

6

'Lines of verse! Lines of rhymed verse!'[14] This is the entirety of one diary entry from the early 1950s. Most of the other poems in Zábrana's collected poems are in free verse. But the poems of *The Lesser Histories* are for the most part tetrameter Petrarchan sonnets. The sonnet is one of the essential forms of the European poetic tradition. Numbering fourteen lines, it was frequently used for long sequences and narratives by poets as various as William Shakespeare, Joachim du Bellay, Elizabeth Barrett Browning, Pierre de Ronsard, Petrarch, and Alexander Pushkin. It could also stand alone, as attested by the work of Robert Frost, William Wordsworth, and John Keats. In the Petrarchan, or Italian, sonnet, the first eight lines set out the mood, scene, or dilemma. And then there is a turn – in Italian, *volta* – as the poet resolves on a course of action, changes their mind, remembers something overlooked; the possibilities are limited only by the sphere of human action and thought. These are not rules to be followed, but rules to be played with. Also, as each century amasses yet further hundreds of the form, there is a burden on the poet to surprise. Thus, a sonneteer, mindful of all the resolutions that have been made after the *volta* in other sonnets, might resolve to do nothing: "They also serve who only stand and wait" (John Milton). If the sonnet was written at a time when sonnets praise the beauty of a lover, then the poet might declare "My mistress' eyes are nothing like the sun" (William Shakespeare). If a lot of preceding sonnets say that the form is a way of preserving the beauty of the lover, then a new sonnet might declare: "Better by far you should forget and smile / Than that you should remember and be sad" (Christina Rosetti). As with many poetic forms, the sonnet with its seemingly strict rules and long tradition, encourages the poet again and again to break these.

---

14   Zábrana, *Celý život*, 163.

By lopping off two syllables from the lines, Zábrana gestures eastward to Russia and Pushkin's Onegin stanza (which is a variation on the sonnet), even as the rhyme form keeps us in the sonnet tradition of the Romance languages. It was a provocative choice in the Czech context of the 1950s. The regime poets rhymed (though they rarely employed the sonnet), while perhaps the most influential unofficial poet of the time, Jiří Kolář, was attempting to write work that avoided traditional form altogether; in this he was inspired by the example of early T. S. Eliot and other Modernists. Kolář held that one could not get to reality through rhyme and metre, which he considered the junk of bygone days. He was one of the key members of Group 42, a movement of painters, theoreticians, and poets who held a similar stance.

The reality that interested Kolář and the other members of the group were the landscapes and people that had been ignored by the pastoral idylls of Czech nationalist literature – among these, Kolář's own native Kladno, an industrial town. They wished to bring into focus what had been previously considered insignificant, the overlooked events of everyday life, unadorned by ideological optimism (whether nationalist or, later, Communist). The critic Jiří Trávníček has written that The Lesser Histories owed much to Group 42's aesthetic (its poems are, after all, pages from a diary, with its implicit idea of documenting everyday life), while the collection also polemicizes with the Group's 'demand that reality take priority, and that it be cleaved to above all.'[15] Kolář and the other members held that:

All technique, genre, and procedures must be broken on reality, since each new moment demands its own new genre, language, and evaluation. However, Zábrana seems to accompany the movement from reality to the poem with a counter movement: may every record find its own and only sonnet, and the sonnet is just as entitled to emboss itself on the record.[16]

---

[15] Jiří Trávníček, Poezie poslední možnosti (Prague: Torst, 1996), 104.

[16] Trávníček, 104.

Readers of Wanda Coleman, Ted Berrigan, or Maurice Scully will recognize Zábrana's impulse here. Zábrana relishes the collision of everyday dross with perhaps the most exalted lyric form in the European poetic tradition. He knew there was something incendiary about his choice. In one diary entry, there is a humorous account of a minor poet coming up to him in a restaurant and exploding:

'You can't do it that way, the way you do it... You can't do that...' At first I didn't know what he was talking about. When I asked what you couldn't 'do that way,' he continued shouting, his voice aggressive, enraged: 'Those sonnets of yours... You can't do it that way, the way you do it... Those enjambments... It doesn't work that way...' The attack was so sudden and incoherent that I couldn't even manage to get upset.[17]

However, that he had annoyed regime poets was only a collateral pleasure of a more serious and considered aesthetic stance. At an earlier moment in the diaries, from the 1950s, he rhetorically asks himself why he rhymes at all. Here is his answer:

I can't just get rid of form with a clean conscience. First I have to degrade it in my own eyes, put it through its paces like a mare, make it trot, canter, and gallop, see if it might not work out after all. I won't buy a car until I've made sure that the mare is lame, blind, and quick to weary.[18]

The passage expresses a care and consideration for the form, but through the violence of the imagery he scruples that its Parnassian luster must be tarnished before use.

Zábrana's stance toward the form itself is also reflected in the content of the poems. For instance, 'Evening Trains' tells of a young man's journey to Prague in 1945, most likely in the summer or fall after the war. Already

---

[17] Zábrana, Celý život, 808.
[18] Zábrana, Celý život, 163.

in the first lines, he registers factories amidst the fields that are rolling by, thus puncturing the obligatory rural idyll of nineteenth-century Czech nationalist writing. The poem also bears the imprint of a particular year when Russian soldiers were in Czechoslovakia, and snatches of their songs would float by on the breeze. By placing this rite of passage in a sonnet (leaving his country home for the city where he would spend the rest of his life), Zábrana might seem to be suggesting this is not momentary but momentous, but the ending dismisses it as a trivial event, as his youth fell away like 'a head of cabbage.' Appearing early in *The Lesser Histories*, Zábrana signals that these sonnets will not build to climactic sententious cadenzas, full of pathos and philosophical dicta. Instead, they will fade back into the mundane, from which they emerged. Another example is 'Right-thinking Women,' mentioned above, about his female co-workers in the factory who are more efficient than he is. Petrarch, and hundreds of subsequent poets, used the sonnet to express female beauty. The fact that Zábrana, then, is using the same form brings an extra sharpness to the poem's irony.

The poems' rhymes are also curious. Poets rhyme in different ways. Marilyn Hacker's rhymes are different from Paul Muldoon's, whose are different again from A. E. Stallings'. Like most rhyming poets, Zábrana has a bassline of fairly standard rhymes. Elsewhere they are macaronic (in 'Evening Trains,' the Russian word *лежит* rhymes with the Czech word *žít*; on the page before, the German word *Heini* rhymes with the Czech word *hájný*), as he delights in the identical sounds that are to be found across languages. Here, on a phonic level, he explores the patterns and dynamics that would govern his life as both a translator from mainly Russian and English, and a citizen of a country caught between the two Cold War powers. Elsewhere, again, the rhymes are hudibrastic, which pairs polysyllabic words with two or three words of one or two syllables. In English, we find the best examples in Lord Byron's *Don Juan* (1819–1824) which rhymes *copy* with *shop. He*, or *heat is* with *Thetis*, and most famously, *intellectual* with *henpecked you all*. The sexism was routine, but the rhyme was not. This expresses a blithe disregard for the rhyming tradition that preceded it (here we might think of the eighteenth-century Augustan poet Thomas Gray who straightforwardly rhymes 'day'/'way', 'lea'/'me', and so on, in his 'Elegy Written in a Country Churchyard'). While Byron used hudibrastic rhyme for knockabout swagger and sport, from another point of view, this kind of rhyme displays an alertness to sound that the previous tradition lacked. It bespeaks a sharp attention to language, finding likenesses where earlier ears heard nothing. Rather than poetic braggadocio, we can also view it as a delicate attunement to the textures of words and inflections. Zábrana sometimes used it to draw attention to a strange accent (as in the last two lines of 'Khlestakov Arrives for Harvest Home, Summer 1945,' which, although the figure in the title is one of Nikolai Gogol's characters, probably refers to the politician Mikuláš Ferjenčík, and how he may have given a Slovak lilt to Czech words). Elsewhere, it creates a tiny hiatus in the idiomatic flow, as in 'Summer 1944,' which rhymes 'toho dne' and 'pohodné.' Zábrana uses this device more variously and more deviously than Byron.

Most frequent of all, however, are three types of rhyme that are strange in Czech. The first is when he steals a syllable from one of the rhyme words, for instance *města/msta* (the second word has only one syllable in Czech); this is the equivalent of rhyming *palace* and *place* in English. The next is a shift in vowel length, as in *drahý/dráhy*; essentially this is a shift in vowel sound, so we might call it pararhyme in English, but a better equivalent might be a shift in stress, as if we paired the noun *rebel* with the verb *to rebel*. And finally he frequently transposes the consonants: *sklap* and *skalp*; *horší* and *hroší*; and *zvětřil zem* and *talířem*.

Provided with a granular account of rhymes that they cannot hear in action, English readers might fairly ask: so what? Is the translator perhaps making an excuse for some of his own awkward maneuvers? The point here is to emphasize the various ways in which Zábrana undermines the

Parnassian flow of traditional rhymes that a reader might have expected to find in a sonnet, while also drawing attention to the subliminal kismet at work in the language that we use each day for both exalted and mundane purposes (and the many in between). His is a heightened attention to our days spent with words, one that remains both faithful to their contours and the poetic forms that house them.

We might also note that 'Evening Trains,' like many others of *The Lesser Histories*, avoids saying 'I,' even though the story it relates is autobiographical. The poems rarely begin with clear declarative states of the annal writer of these lesser histories (an earlier working title of the book was *The Annals*). Rather they start by seeming to catch from the air a few odd skeins of feeling that might belong to anyone, along with snatches of overheard songs. The sonnet barely seems to be orchestrating its materials: rather it collects them the way that leaves and small bits of trash might gather in a neglected building entrance. It is as though Zábrana sets up the form of the sonnet, and simply waits to see what will catch in it. We might draw another analogy to a sound artist who strolls around a city holding out a microphone. In the twentieth and twenty-first centuries, poetic form is typecast as a bully, blindly imposing its will upon reality, and thus reducing rich complexity to jingling rhymes and beat-machine rhythms. *The Lesser Histories*, made up of crafted tetrameter Petrarchan sonnets, gives the lie to this stereotype.

7

In 1999, Jay-Z recorded a song entitled 'Big Pimpin'' that employed a sample from the song 'Khosara Khosara' (1957) by the Egyptian musician Baligh Hamdi. This led to some legal tussles, but despite the repeated and protracted court cases that arise from sampling, hip-hop artists will not let the technique go. Why? One critic, Rory Seydel, has said it triggers our memories: hearing a new song that includes a sample of a song that is ten or fifteen years old can flood the present with the emotions and experiences of a previous period;[19] so a good hip-hop artist will have both an exhaustive knowledge of the canon and an astute apprehension of what their audience will and will not remember. Seydel points out that sampling can serve another purpose – the inverse of the preceding one – when it uses songs that are unknown to the audience. This is a way of drawing attention to work that is unfamiliar either because it is from another culture (Hamdi is an example of this) or because it has been forgotten by the hip-hop artist's own culture (for instance, Beyoncé's sample of The Chi-Lites' 'Are You My Woman (Tell Me So)' [1971] in her song 'Crazy in Love' [2003]). We might add that there's another category of songs that are famous for being sampled (David McCallum's 'The Edge' [1967] has been sampled over thirty times by artists such as Quasimoto, Kevin Gates, Missin Linx, Kendrick Lamar, all of whom are probably alluding to its early sample by Dr. Dre and Snoop Dog in 'The Next Episode' [2000]).

Sampling has a long pedigree in literature, and *The Lesser Histories* employs the technique widely – in epigraphs, allusions, and segues into quotes from the work of other writers; sometimes these last are marked by italics or quotes, and other times the maneuver is seamless. A diary entry of 1980 reflects upon the citations in *The Lesser Histories*:

> The citations – other people's formulations, used or abused – entered into the poems themselves, without forethought, simply with the same degree of insistence they had in my own consciousness. If everyday things are present for you, if they are the subject of your work with words – and for me they always are and will be; a professional translator would have to be a dead stump overgrown with moss for them not to be – then words will eventually change into a part of your reality. They'll be just as real as a light switch on the wall, a rainy day outside the window, the carpet beneath your feet.... Such words, such combinations or chains of words, will then shine anew – they are now 'dressed up,' stepping into 'society' in a jester's costume or in a tuxedo, in overalls or a bathing suit; they smell of perfume, or

[19] Rory Seydel, "Why You Should Stop Thinking of Sampling as Theft," *Landr* (Jun. 20, 2016) https://blog.landr.com/sampling-isnt-theft/. Accessed Feb. 17, 2021.

of the shit they just stepped in. Such words carry two or three times the weight – they drag along a baggage of emotion, something that words don't have when they're taken from linear reality... Such verses then become a collection of golden and rainbow-colored flies in amber.[20]

Dylan Thomas, Boris Pasternak, John Donne, Alexander Pushkin, William Carlos Williams, Osip Mandelstam, and C. Day Lewis are attributed openly in *The Lesser Histories*, while the reader will have to be spry to catch Viktor Shklovsky (the last two lines of 'Jealousy'), *The Bartered Bride* (the title of 'A Graceful Little Bear'), and the late nineteenth-century Czech poet Josef Machar (the title of 'Here Should Blossom'). Zábrana himself sometimes forgot which sources he had used. (Did he pick up the Latin phrase, '*Prodeunt vexilla regum,* – which was translated to make the title of 'Banners of Kings' – during his schooldays in Humpolec? Years later he discovered that it was in fact from the period 1950–1952 when he studied theology.[21]) Somewhat like the Dr. Dre example above, he used a quote from Alexander Pushkin's poem of the same title for 'Demons'; this had also served as the epigraph to Fyodor Dostoyevsky's later novel, of the same title. Zábrana also draws upon fragments of overheard conversation or conversations the poet himself is involved in ('TV Screen,' 'Midnight Monolog,' 'Golden Scalp,' 'Ungallant Conversation'). 'Tabloid Reader' is a cento of truncated quotes from tabloid newspapers, while 'Black Morning Memory' ends with two scraps of sentences from a diary found in a trash can.

So, the borders of this lyric subject are porous. In the anglophone world at present, translation is often considered secondary to creative work, a level below the writing of fiction or poetry. This is a relatively recent idea,

---

[20]   Zábrana, *Celý život*, 740.
[21]   Zábrana, *Celý život*, 582. I'm grateful to Martin Pokorný for pointing out to me that this appears in Canto 34 of Dante's *Inferno*. It is originally from the Latin hymn, 'Vexilla Regis,' which, like the Dr. Dre sample, was subsequently alluded to in works by Gustav Holst, James Joyce, and David Jones.

stemming from Romanticism, and it can obscure the profound and inventive imaginative engagement involved in translation. To understand Zábrana the poet, we also have to understand how translation was fundamental to his poetry. This comes through clearly in his use of quotations. More generally, we are reading poems that are generously open to other poems; indeed, one might say that the poet is in part *made* by other voices.

This can seem counterintuitive. Poetry is so often figured as the voice of the individual spirit, or as self-expression; such a description won't work for *The Lesser Histories*, which at times resembles a loose, shifting congregation of voices, some talking clearly, others muttering indistinctly, on occasion shifting from one language to another. In English, we might be tempted to draw an analogy with T. S. Eliot's *The Waste Land* (Zábrana knew this work), but Marianne Moore's samplings of conversations, classics, tourist brochures, and government publications in a poem like 'An Octopus' is a better fit. Zábrana's poem 'Short Circuit' has an epigraph from Mandelstam's poem, 'Oh, how we love to play the hypocrite,' and the last two lines are a translation of part of the epigraph. But if you can't read Cyrillic, you'll miss it, as the shift in authorship is not marked. (We face the same uncertainty in translations from a language we don't know: how much of the style and the tone of what we are reading belongs to the translator and how much to the author?) Who, then, speaks here? If these are pages from a diary, then whose diary is it? At this juncture, it is a Czech-Russian persona, as Zábrana ever so slightly takes on the aspect of the banned, imprisoned Mandelstam; so, the Russian expands transnationally, finding purchase in Czech culture. Also, two periods are intermixed, the early 1930s when the Russian poem was written, and the 1950s, when 'Short Circuit' was most likely first drafted. It turns out that we are reading the diary of much more than one person.

These subliminal transitions might make readers feel that they are taking an examination rather than reading poetry. Who is supposed to get all these references? What reader knows the Czech literary tradition, as well

as Russian, German, and English in the originals? While the Czech read-
er might be expected to recognize some of the broader contours of the
country's history in the twentieth century, as well as be able to make out
Cyrillic and some of the German (at least in Zábrana's time), they will often
be pulled up short by Zábrana's allusions to episodes in his personal life.
In turn, an English reader of poetry will perhaps (but not necessarily) be
familiar with Dylan Thomas and William Carlos Williams (though, probably,
no longer C. Day Lewis), but hazy on the Czech background.

We saw above how hip-hop artists work subtly with the broader cultur-
al memory of their audience, by turns flattering, teasing, and intriguing lis-
teners. Those who get it right can play this cultural memory like a grand in-
strument. Often, while translating Zábrana's poems, I encountered a word
or phrase that was unknown to most Czech speakers younger than 80, as it
was the slang of a bygone age; and many of those readers might not catch
the exact luster of a quote from William Carlos Williams or Dylan Thomas.
Often it can seem that there is no overlap between the groups of people
who will get different passages of the poems. Who, then, is the intended
reader of these poems, but a man who grew up in a Czech country town,
moved to Prague, was scarred by the regime during his teens, worked as
a translator from Russian and English? Who, except Zábrana himself?

Indeed, the thousand pages or so of his selected diaries bears witness
to a splendid if bitter solitude. But many entries are clearly written for an
ideal reader, and not Zábrana himself. Perhaps these readers were in the
past, perhaps in the future, and Zábrana's keeps faith with them. Some of
the poems may at first seem like vatic whispers uttered at a frequency we
cannot catch, but Zábrana *published* this book, and as we lean in closer to
these sonnets, we realize that he wanted them to be overheard.

CONTENTS

TRANSLATOR'S ACKNOWLEDGEMENTS

Some of these translations were first published in *BODY*, *Fortnightly Review*, *New York Review of Books*, *Modern Poetry in Translation*, and *Plume*; a shorter version of the afterword was published in the *Los Angeles Review of Books*. I am grateful to the Czech Literary Center and the Moravian Library for a fellowship that enabled me to spend a fortnight in Brno completing a first draft. Petr Onufer first put a copy of Zábrana's poems in my hand in a pub near Flora; Petr Šrámek gave me a copy of the poems as a gift: these are significant debts. I would also like to thank Josef Hrdlička, Hynek Janoušek, Alistair Noon, Adéla Petruželková, Jana Prikryl, Františka Schormová, Michael Špirit, Jan Šulc, Brad Vice, Marie Zábranová, and above all Jonathan Bolton, Tereza Límanová, and Martin Pokorný.

Jan Zábrana
THE LESSER HISTORIES

Translated by Justin Quinn

KAROLINUM PRESS
Karolinum Press is a publishing department of Charles University
Ovocný trh 560/5, 116 36 Prague 1, Czech Republic
www.karolinum.cz

Cover and design by Jiří Voves
Set and printed in the Czech Republic by Karolinum Press
First English edition

ISBN 978-80-246-4933-7
ISBN 978-80-246-4934-4 (pdf)
ISBN 978-80-246-4935-1 (epub)
ISBN 978-80-246-4936-8 (mobi)

MODERN CZECH CLASSICS

Published titles
Zdeněk Jirotka: *Saturnin* (2003, 2005, 2009, 2013; pb 2016)
Vladislav Vančura: *Summer of Caprice* (2006; pb 2016)
Karel Poláček: *We Were a Handful* (2007; pb 2016)
Bohumil Hrabal: *Pirouettes on a Postage Stamp* (2008)
Karel Michal: *Everyday Spooks* (2008)
Eduard Bass: *The Chattertooth Eleven* (2009)
Jaroslav Hašek: *Behind the Lines: Bugulma and Other Stories*
(2012; pb 2016)
Bohumil Hrabal: *Rambling On* (2014; pb 2016)
Ladislav Fuks: *Of Mice and Mooshaber* (2014)
Josef Jedlička: *Midway upon the Journey of Our Life* (2016)
Jaroslav Durych: *God's Rainbow* (2016)
Ladislav Fuks: *The Cremator* (2016)
Bohuslav Reynek: *The Well at Morning* (2017)
Viktor Dyk: *The Pied Piper* (2017)
Jiří R. Pick: *Society for the Prevention of Cruelty to Animals* (2018)
*Views from the Inside: *Czech Underground Literature and Culture
(1948–1989)*, ed. M. Machovec (2018)
Ladislav Grosman: *The Shop on Main Street* (2019)
Bohumil Hrabal: *Why I Write? The Early Prose from 1945 to 1952* (2019)
*Jiří Pelán: Bohumil Hrabal: *A Full-length Portrait* (2019)
*Martin Machovec: *Writing Underground* (2019)
Ludvík Vaculík: *A Czech Dreambook* (2019)
Jaroslav Kvapil: *Rusalka* (2020)
Jiří Weil: *Lamentation for 77,297 Victims* (2021)
Vladislav Vančura: *Ploughshares into Swords* (2021)
Siegfried Kapper: *Tales from the Prague Ghetto* (2022)

Forthcoming
Jan Procházka: *Ear*
Ivan M. Jirous: *End of the World. Poetry and Prose*
Jan Čep: *Common Rue*
Jiří Weil: *Moscow – Border*
Libuše Moníková: *Verklärte Nacht*

MODERN SLOVAK CLASSICS

Forthcoming
Ján Johanides: *But Crimes Do Punish* (2022)

*Scholarship

Milá Jarmilo,

ty má dobrá duše,
když tě dopis jneváš
potěšil, ale odpověd
psát nemohl, jsem str-
sklíchý a vyčerpaný i te-
en bohon, dávají mi
a vážím 69 kg i bol

K té anarchii:
Balet má 2 poida
D Pavník